School

BY KATHY THORNBOROUGH • ILLUSTRATIONS BY KATHLEEN PETELINSEK

The Child's World®

A SPECIAL THANKS TO OUR ADVISERS:

As a member of a deaf family that spans four generations, Kim Bianco Majeri lives, works, and plays amongst the deaf community.

Carmine L. Vozzolo is an educator of children who are deaf and hard of hearing, as well as their families.

PUBLISHED by The Child's World®
1980 Lookout Drive • Mankato, MN 56003-1705
800-599-READ • www.childsworld.com

ACKNOWLEDGMENTS
The Child's World®: Mary Berendes, Publishing Director
The Design Lab: Design
Jody Jensen Shaffer: Editing

PHOTO CREDITS
© Ansis Klucis/Shutterstock.com: back cover, 7; BrandX: 14, 16, 18, 19, 21, 23; DoctorKan/iStock.com: 5; gbh007/iStock.com: 13; Garnhamphotography/iStock.com: 20; Igor Lateci/Shutterstock.com: 11; iofoto iStock.com: 9; Ivansabo/Dreamstime.com: 22; Kadak/Shutterstock.com: 3; Kalina Vova/Dreamstime.com: 15; LanKS /Shutterstock.com: 12; omgimages/iStock.com: 10; PhotoDisc: 17; Quang Ho/Shutterstock.com: 8; SLP_London/Shutterstock.com: back cover, 6; Veronica Louro/Shutterstock.com: cover, 1, 4

ISBN 9781626873223
LCCN 2014934500

PRINTED in the United States of America
Mankato, MN
August, 2014
PA02248

NOTE TO PARENTS AND EDUCATORS:

The understanding of any language begins with the acquisition of vocabulary, whether the language is spoken or manual. The books in the Talking Hands series provide readers, both young and old, with a first introduction to basic American Sign Language signs. Combining close photocues and simple, but detailed, line illustrations, children and adults alike can begin the process of learning American Sign Language. Let these books be an introduction to the world of American Sign Language. Most languages have regional dialects and multiple ways of expressing the same thought. This is also true for sign language. We have attempted to use the most common version of the signs for the words in this series. As with any language, the best way to learn is to be taught in person by a frequent user. It is our hope that this series will pique your interest in sign language.

Bus

See page 24 to learn how to make all the letters.

Spell B-U-S with your fingers.

3

School

Face your palms together as shown.
Clap your hands together twice.

What is your favorite class?

Class

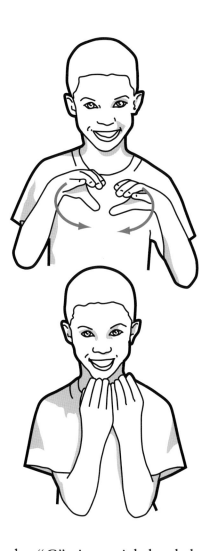

Make the "C" sign with both hands facing each other. Then roll your wrists so that your pinkies touch.

Backpack

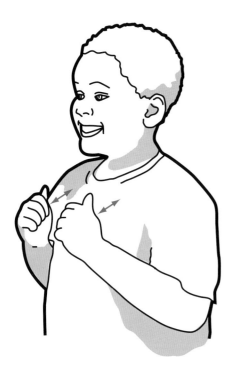

Tap your chest with your thumbs.

Backpacks are also called "rucksacks" or "knapsacks."

Desk

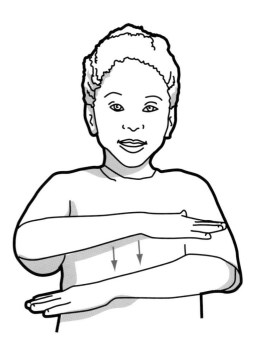

Move your right arm down
and tap your left arm twice.

Students began
using desks in
school in the 1880s.

7

Chair

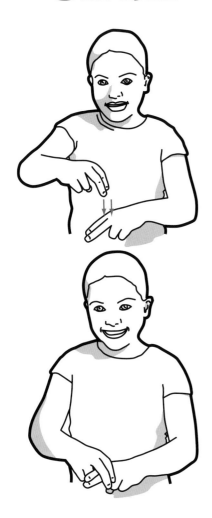

Tap your right index and middle fingers over your left index and middle fingers twice.

Chairs did not become common until the 1500s.

Raising your hand is the right way to ask a question in class.

Student

Close your fingers together as you move your hand toward your forehead. Then face palms together and motion downward.

9

Teacher

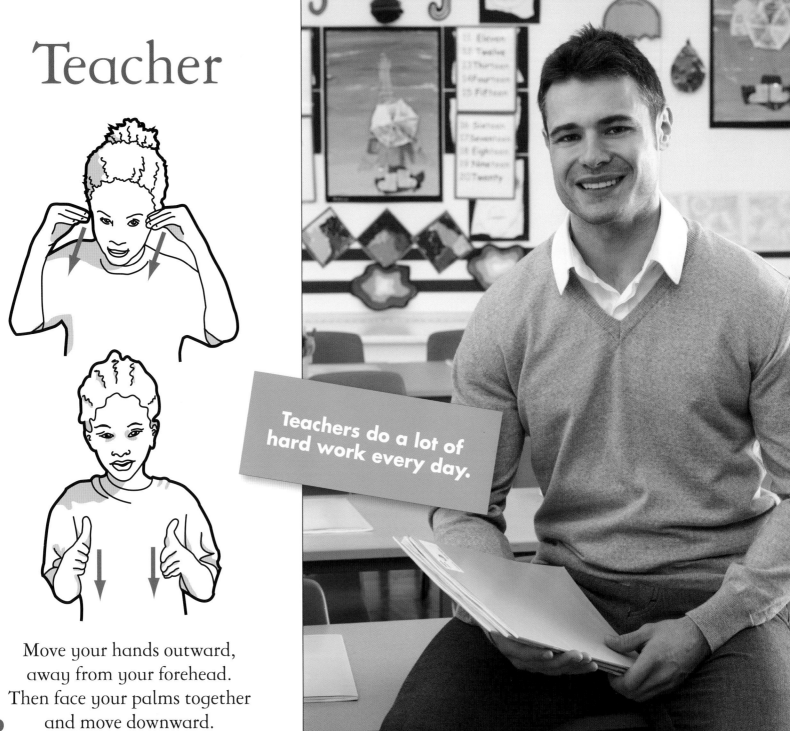

Move your hands outward,
away from your forehead.
Then face your palms together
and move downward.

Teachers do a lot of
hard work every day.

Computer

Many computers today are laptops, like this one.

Make the letter "C" with your right hand. Brush your thumb twice on your left arm.

Book

Open your hands as if you are opening a book.

What is your favorite book?

Library

Make the letter "L" and circle clockwise.
(The person you are speaking to
will see the sign go counterclockwise.)

There are more than 120,000 libraries in the United States.

Pencil

Touch your fingers to your mouth.
Then pretend to write on your left hand.

The idea for wooden pencils started about 500 years ago.

Paper

Have both hands flat. Face your palms together and sweep your right hand across your left hand, toward your body. Repeat.

Paper is made from mashed wood or grasses.

Paint

Move your right hand up and down against your left hand as if you were using a paintbrush.

Paint has been around for about 100,000 years.

Glue

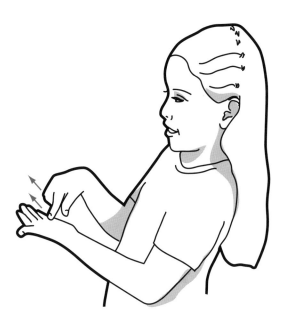

Make the letter "G" with your right hand. Move your fingers along your flat left hand from the palm to the fingers.

Some people like glue for projects. Others like paste.

GLue

DO NOT EAT

2.5 NET OZS.

Scissors

Move your fingers like scissors.

Scissors have been around for about 500 years.

Eraser

Make a fist. Move it over your flat left hand as if you are erasing something.

Erasers are made from rubber.

Crayons

Wiggle all your fingers a little by your mouth. Then pretend to write on your hand.

Crayons are made of wax. If they get hot enough, they can melt.

Bell

Your finger hits your flat hand.

The part of a bell that makes the sound is called the "clapper."

Playground

Make the "Y" shape with both hands. Flick them twice. Then with your right hand, make a flat circle.

Some people call a playground a "park," or "play area."

Clock

Tap your wrist. Then hold both hands up by your face.

Does the clock in your classroom look like this?

A SPECIAL THANK YOU!

A special thank you to our models from the Program for Children Who are Deaf and Hard of Hearing at the Alexander Graham Bell Elementary School in Chicago, Illinois.

Alina's favorite things to do are art, soccer, and swimming. DJ is her brother!

Dareous likes football. His favorite team is the Detroit Lions. He also likes to play video games.

Darionna likes the swings and merry-go-round on the playground. She also loves art.

DJ loves playing the harmonica and video games. Alina is his sister!

Jasmine likes writing and math in school. She also loves to swim.

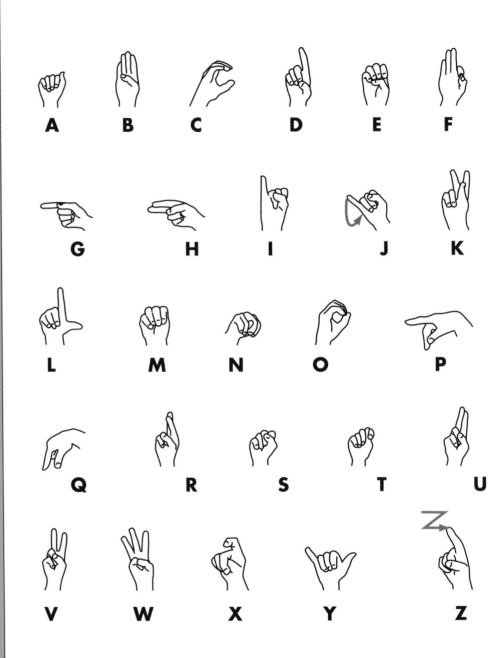